Relationships:
Transitioning from
Significant
Other to Spouse

Relationships:
Transitioning from Significant Other to Spouse

Eugene Barnes

Rivers of Water Publishing Co.
Rocky Mount, North Carolina 27804

Rivers of Water Publishing Co.
Robin M. Manley, Owner
Rocky Mount, NC 27804
www.rowpublishing.webs.com
redbrd007@hotmail.com
rowpub2017@gmail.com

This book is a work of non-fiction inspired by real life
experiences. The contents of this books are created by the
author, based on what he has observed in his past relationships
and the relationships of many others. No names are mentioned,
other than to give credit to famous singers of whose songs that
are briefly mentioned. The name of significant others which are
mentioned are done so with expressed permission. The contents
of this book include the author's personal opinion, but the
author does not claim to be an expert, nor does he hold any
professional licensures or degrees in the subject matter. All
scriptures are quoted from the New King James Version of the
Holy Bible unless otherwise noted. Anyone needing
professional counseling for relationship issues should not rely
on this book as main source of counseling, but rather consider
it the unprofessional opinion of the author. Any definition of
words is taken from the online Merriam-Webster dictionary.

Design by: Robin M. Manley
ISBN 978-1-947513-01-3
Library of Congress Control Number: 2017962740   F
First Edition

Acknowledgements

Not one person in life is ever successful without the corporate effort of many gifted people, who are willing to iterate and submit their talents, skills, and experience for others. Everyone is the total outcome of all the people we have met and learned from. This work is the product of countless people whose thoughts, ideas, good times, and sad times has reveal to me the knowledge that I have placed in this book.

Periodically, I will use the term educational truth/s, because I have been truly educated from other people's ups and downs, as well as my own. I want to thank Betty, my wife. Now, she was not my wife at the beginning of this work, but we did transition from significant other to spouse before this book was complete. So, thank you Betty for being patient with my long-drawn-out hours of study and attentiveness to this book. My achievements are yours as well.

Dr. Robin Manley, owner of Rivers of Water Publishing Co., thank you for your deep commitment and dedication. Robin has proven to be one of the most encouraging, inspirational, and motivational individuals in bringing thoughts, ideas, and concepts together. It is her professional knowledge of publishing and penmanship required that made this work possible. Due to your loyalty and trust of my reputation as a potential author, you invested your time into helping with publishing this book; therefore, you are an author's dream and a gift to the trusted millions who will read this book. The blessings of God are taking you where the world system cannot touch you. The God-giving ability in your life has been a tremendous impact on mines. Again, thank you.

Dr. Robin is a nickname given to Robin by Eugene Barnes. As of April 2018, she does not have her doctorate's degree (PhD).

Last, but certainly not least, I would like to acknowledge my pastor and mentor, Dr. Bernard Grant, who has confirmed many of the thoughts that I have concerning relationships. I cannot help but listen whenever I'm in his presence. The Bible says, "A wise man will hear to increase his learning and a man of understanding will attain unto wise counsel" (*Proverbs 1:5, KJV*). The Amplified Bible says, "The wise also will hear and increase in learning, and the person of understanding will acquire skills and attain to be sound counsel, so that he may be able to steer his course rightly.

The way Dr. Grant brings his congregation from sickness to health, poverty to wealth, mediocrity to metority, Turkey to Eagles, darkness to light, and from hatred to love, is with his God-given ability to teach us by rightly dividing the word of truth.

Dr. Bernard Grant, I'm proud to have you as my pastor, mentor, and spiritual father. Thank you for caring and sharing with us what God has given you. Eugene Barnes

Dedications

There couldn't be a better time in my life to present this book to my wife. If you buy a book to read, it's likely that you will read the title first. Well, if you did, then that is exactly what has happened between starting and finishing this part of what is more to come.

Yes! We have transitioned from significant other to spouse. My wife, Betty Lou is the typical example and representative of womanhood. She is an absolute paragon of peace and the utopia of feminism, and I don't mean in Greek mythology, contrary to the Merriam-Webster's opinion.

Preface

The material in this book is about relationships. It is *'the way in which two or more concepts, objects, or people are connected.'* I have made this statement many times in the past. "You can't beat two people working together." Therefore, you must see you and your significant other has a team. People do need people. If you can't include your significant other, then you are with the wrong person. You must practice that relationship teamwork. And you do that by teamwork communicating, teamwork-apologies, teamwork forgiveness, teamwork-honesty, meaning no hidden secrets. Andrew Carnegie once said, "Teamwork is the ability to work together towards a common vision. It is the ability to direct individual accomplishments towards organizational objectives, which is the fuel that allows common people to attain uncommon results." So, work hard with your mate by apologizing when you are wrong and forgiving when he or she is wrong. If one wants to communicate and the other one doesn't, one will apologize and the other one won't. It is not the kind of communication fuel that will keep the relationship-plane in flight. My theory is: the first to apologize is the bravest; the first to forgive is the strongest, and the first to forget about it, is the happiest. I promise you.

One will apologize and the other will not, is mutually inconclusive. Many relationships in time past has gone sour because of gossip. Keep in mind that gossip will not benefit neither of the three; (1.) the one being talked about, (2.) the one doing the talking, or (3.) the one giving a listening ear to that garbage.

I concluded that a Wilson, North Carolina attorney's relationship with his client to be L.I.C. (Lunely Illegally Cartoonist). Some people will spend any amount from $50 to $5,000,000 on a wedding and not five minutes to keep their marriage together. So, as you read this book, you will see that many of these educational truths is not criticism, not on my part, but simply some critical observations. It includes people from all walks of life and from every direction, from innocent to bizarre and dissident; from the meek to the most cantankerous; from the weakest to the most barbaric; from dysfunctional to professional; and from the most fragile minds to the most profound. Simply because of these observations, I can honestly say that my life isn't predicted upon the accolades, philosophies, and dictates of other people's opinions and ideas, but only on the uncompromising engrafted, sin detoxing, stupendously impressive Holy Word of God that can and will help you establish a comfortable atmosphere in the very midst of adversity. The mountains and valleys in life are most definitely inevitable in every relationship, but there are ways of getting things right and keeping them right. If you are sincere and you want to, there may be a few things in this book which will show you how to get them right.

Remember: A small flower every now and then can keep a big fight a bay. ~ *Eugene Barnes*

Introduction

I remember reading in the 1989 World Almanac (if I'm accurate) about the marriage statistics in every state in America. North Carolina had more than 50,000 marriages that year (1989). North Carolina also had more than 30,000 divorces. Do you know that 89% of those 30,000 divorces were because of financial insecurities as opposed to infidelity? However, infidelity was also a cause of divorce. Now, let me explain the principal point. It may be a little rhetorical, but financial insecurities and infidelity has destroyed many marriages. It has turned many simple discussable matters into debatable issues. It has turned sweet, sweet camaraderie into highly ungodly rhetoric and nothing relevant regarding peace. It leads to an atmosphere conducive to verbal abuse, if not physical violence, but in many cases, both.

In order to improve relationships and lower the divorce rate we must learn what happened to the respect once given in relationships and work on bringing it back.

Eugene Barnes

What Happened to Respect?

We live in a society with no respect because of a lack of love, trust, and commitment to our spouse or significant other. What has happened to respect? Living in a world of unlimited choices and possibilities is what makes it so difficult to say, "I love you and you only."

If your lover is telling you that he or she loves you and telling someone else the same thing while with you, then he or she is either lying to one of you or loving both of you with a partial heart and neither one of you with his or her whole heart. Now, I believe it is possible to love two people, but you will obligate and commit yourself to only one.

In the 1950's, there was a singing group called the Platters. This group sang a song entitled *Only You.* Some of the lyrics went something like this:

> *Only you can make this world seem right.*
> *Only you can make the darkness bright.*
> *Only you and you alone can thrill me like you do,*
> *and it feels so good to love just only you.*

Only you can make this change in me.
Oh, oh, oh! It's true, you are my destiny.
When I hold your hand, I understand the magic that
you do and it thrills my heart to love just only you.

Those are just a few of the lyrics that I remember and I think they are great. The lyrics in many of these songs make you wonder what those women were like (if they were singing about one particular woman). God's divine ability to create, stack, form, and shape women has held us in awe and has stunned men with both fantasy and reality for centuries. On the other hand, there are those, men and women alike, who has made an incredible display of their ignorance and stupidity. We just can't commit. We just can't obligate ourselves to a significant other, much less a spouse.

Now, I do understand that some people just aren't marriage material. However, from a Biblical point of view, you are marriage material, if you are lust material. **If** is mentioned in the Bible three hundred and thirty (331) times. *If* is a functional word used to introduce an exclamatory phrase, a supposition meaning, suppose that uncertain possibility, conditions, or stipulation occurs.

If is a functional word used to introduce an exclamatory phrase, a supposition meaning, suppose that uncertain possibility, conditions or stipulation occurs.

We are under the moral restraints of God's righteous grace. The unimaginable heartbreak of a loss can be devastating, whether it is death or divorce.

Now, I'm sure there are more cases like the one I'm about to mention, but I know of a case in which a man punched his wife. It was a terrible blow. The punch wasn't fatal, but definitely bodacious and unforgettable. Well, do you know what was more stupid than him punching her? The fact that she never left. When the police arrived the husband and wife gave all the details about the fussing and fighting. One of the police officers noticed a scar on the upper part of the wife's forehead, near her hairline.

"Where did you get that scar?" The officer asked the woman.

It looked as if it had been healed for a while.

"He did that about five-years ago," she replied.

"This same guy? The officer asked, referring to the man who had punched her.

"Yes," she replied.

"How much more of this can you take?" The officer asked the woman. "I have concluded that you're not a smart lady by a long shot. He may have knocked away part of your brain five-years ago," the officer said.

My question to the reader is, "What is your relationship like? Is it getting bitter or better?" I hope it is getting better all the time. Issues of domestic violence has gone on for such a long time, but that doesn't make it right and from God's point of view, it is Biblically inexcusable.

If your relationship is crumbling, then ask yourself why? Was it a lack of truth? Did you keep searching for new information about your new mate which you should have asked him or her yourself? If you didn't trust him or her to tell you the truth, then you should not have embarked upon this relationship from the beginning.

Is it true love?

If there is true love, sacrifice can never be too great, but saying, 'I love you,' can be too late if you don't stay on top of things. What kinds of things? Things like keeping the acid out of your relationship. Anything that is causing problems in your relationship is like acid on your clothes; it will eat them up. Problems in a relationship will breakdown the relationship. When your relationship is in intensive care, when your relationship is on life support, ask yourself, "What do I do to resurrect this relationship?" Remember that your aggressiveness in attempting to resurrect the relationship may lead to more heartbreak. Keep in mind the reason for the break-up in the first place. As in the situation I mentioned earlier, which involved the police, some of your brain may have been knocked out already. You see, the human mind is multi-disciplinary and is a very sophisticated mechanism in exercising its ability to perceive. Multi-disciplinary which means, composed of or combining several usually separate branches of learning or fields of expertise.

So, protect your mind physically, as well as emotionally. You have no right to keep your head between those two slices of bread, only to be called an idiot sandwich. Stop beating yourself up.

Many relationships

Multi-disciplinary: composed of /or combining several usually separate branches of learning or fields of expertise

are shabby because it started with one or the other trying to love the one he or she is with because he or she couldn't be with the one he or she love.

Maybe this is the reason many spouses and significant others double back to their ex whenever possible. If that happens, leave them there. Now, I'm not suggesting that every time there's bickering, the relationship is over, but use a little wisdom. "Is it worth it?"

Let the super-star in you come out and you can do that apart from being egotistical. You are a very important specimen. The Bible says that we are fearfully and wonderfully made and that we are a peculiar people. It must be a critical economical dependency to chase after someone after being told that the relationship is over. It's as stupid as trying to drown a fish or trying to catch a cab with a fishing pole. You don't need clandestine operations in your life. The only problem in life is those

| Clandestine: is things held in secrecy or concealment, subversion or deception. |

horrible people and things that you just can't seem to let go of and those people and things that has made a bold barbaric display of exposing misery in your life. Could that be the reason why you never congregate to communicate with other people?

Yeah! I know-I know! Your ego has been assaulted and left vulnerable to shame and in many cases, criticism. Stability is sometimes hard to maintain in the very best of relationships, but it will be successful if they both really want it to. Just remember what I stated earlier about 'if.' Whatever you do, just don't allow yourself to constitute moral or immoral restraints to hold on to anybody. Don't ever do that! Why would you do something like that? It's a terrible miscarriage of logic and a devastating climax of mental immorality. As ego gratifying as love is, you must remember this, "You're indubitably stunning! You're impressively striking! You're not only the utopia of feminism, but humanity!

Will it last?

Let me enlighten you briefly on where you stand

as *utopia of feminism.*

Utopia: an imagined place or state of things in which everything is perfect.

Remember, names mean
something. Utopia means
perfection. A look at utopia
can be found in a book
written by Sir Thomas

More in 1516, entitled Utopia. This book
describes an imaginary island which enjoys a
system of political and social perfection. Utopia is
a hard standard to live up to.

Speaking of Utopia! A club name Utopia
once opened in Wilson, North Carolina. When the
club opened, my prediction was that it wouldn't last
18-months. Why did I make that prediction? My
prediction wasn't because I assumed there would be
poor management, nor did I have anything against
the club owner. My prediction about the club's
success was based on the crowd that was drawn to

the club and I predicted there would be beggars. Out of the 125 cars of people who attended the club, only 30 cars of people would actually be spending money. Doesn't the perfection of a club environment include crowds of people coming and spending money each night? The name Utopia implied perfection; however, do you think it was accomplished? What was missing in the relationship between the materials needed for the club, the customers, and what was expected based on the name of the clubs-Utopia? How relationships work together does matter. It's important to handle each relationship to the best of your ability or perfection. I'm just explaining the *utopia* and your importance in a relationship. Now, relationships are relationships, intimate or casual, but we must be taught to handle relationships casually on the front side of life, long before we can encounter any intimacy. Oh, by the way, the Utopia club lasted 20-months. Remember, it's *good* that ultimately triumphs over *evil* and *virtue* that will be rewarded in your relationship? Keep the optimism, and be wise enough to realize when the relationship is starting to misfire like bad spark plugs. Try to eliminate the misfires. The more downtime and breakups between you and your significant other; the less chance of a final relationship resurrection. The only optimistic one is you. The only enthusiastic one is you. If he isn't expressing his feelings for you or she isn't expressing her feelings for you, why do you think you must always be the aggressor? It could be that you're not the only link in his or her chain? Do you remember the song Aretha Franklin sung years ago, 'Chain, Chain?

> **Optimism-** hopefulness and confidence about the future or the successful outcome of something. **Pessimism-** a tendency to see the worst aspect of things or believe that the worst will happen; a lack of hope or confidence in the future.

> *'I'm just a link in your chain.*
> *You treat me mean.*
> *Oh, you treat me cruel.'*

What is it that your significant others could be saying behind your back? I know of a case in which a man had been telling his "so-called" significant other how much he really, really loved her. At the same time, he was seeing her, he was telling the guys that she had been passed around more times than a bottle of cheap whiskey.

Now, I don't know what her attitude was like, her educational background, character disposition, or ancestral pedigree, but if she is looking like a decent woman, ready to make a change, and looking you square in your eye pupils and telling you that she loves only you, then you make sure that you and her, whether at her house, your house, or a restaurant, next meal is a "Happy Meal." Ronald McDonald has nothing to do with this.

You have the God-given ability to raise each other from pessimism to optimism, from mediocre to extraordinary, or from Vienna sausages to ribeye steak. Hey man, help that woman raise her spirit from agony to ecstasy. Help her climb the stretching academic Alps, to the pinnacle of optimal potential and possibilities. Help him climb to untold heights, leaps, and bounds.

Do you understand the word, "megalo-mania?" It refers to a highly exaggerated delusional concept of your own importance. The delusional doesn't sound that exciting, but other parts of the definition means, "an outburst of wildly extravagant. In a failing relationship case, this could be a wonderful thing.

Did you tell her that she is the most enchanting, (the typical example and representative of womanhood)? Tell her that she makes the mundane absolutely phenomenal (highly extraordinary and exceptional). I'm sure she would like to hear it. You see, a woman is moved by spoken words, but the average man is moved by sight. He sees the physical and goes off. She hears the verbal and is impressed (If there is any or little creditability to what's being said, if there is any trustworthiness of speech). In other words, he sees, she listens. Personally, I don't think that's all bad.

Well, I don't claim to be the great pedantic pedagogue, dogmatic, or formal, but I've been around long enough to learn just a few things.

Mistake or Choice

What's considered bad behavior in a relationship? One of the main things is cheating on your spouse or significant other and calling it a mistake, rather than a few bad choices. Yeah! That's right, a few bad choices. If you cheat on your spouse or significant other one time, it would require a few bad choices. You didn't make a mistake when you flirted with her, asked for her phone number, met her, and then slept with her. That many mistakes in your relationships leaves me far from being shocked.

Now before I married Betty Lou, I was married a total of thirty-eight years between two other women, nineteen years with each woman. There was a two-year break in between the first two marriages. I was a man who was married thirty-eight undistinguished, meaningless, pointless, failed laden, and dilapidated years. I want to say that every single day of those thirty-eight years was like climbing a towering inferno of horror and terror. It was disgusting, despicable, and I felt much misery and despair for what I accomplished.

There was a time when I was a man with a chip on my shoulder the size of the national debt. Yeah! I was a bitter, sour, friendless, and a cold-hearted evil man, not to mention I was a grasping compulsive. My outcome was equivalent to a Vietnam vet. I was haunted by flash-backs and nightmarish visions until I was unable to separate reality from the horrific world into which I had lapsed.

My previous two marriages were not mistakes, but bad choices. The Bible says, *"For all have sinned and come short of the glory of God"* (Romans 3:23, KJV). It didn't say 'all have made mistakes,' (although we have), but God said, "all have sinned and come short of His glory." Sin is a choice. Oh, by the way, mistakes are very brief misunderstandings, mis-conceptions, and/or insufficient knowledge; whereas, a choice is the act of choosing to select or having the power and right to do so.

Making a decision is not hardly a mistake of the second definition. Do you agree? Anyway, the second definition is much more likely to lead to violence and dispute than the first decision. I do believe that there is just as much difference between a choice and a mistake as there is between the Gettysburg Address and a welcome speech. The Gettysburg Address was a short speech made by President Lincoln on November 19, 1863. The speech was made during the dedication of the National Cemetery at Gettysburg, but still much longer and more sacred than a welcome speech, but no more popular because of the hospitality, although lacking in longevity.

I said all of that to be understood. Hope you got the message about behavior. Now, when speaking of behavior, especially the wicked and unethical behavior, we are making reference to that which is unprincipled, unscrupulous, dishonorable, deceitful, fraudulent, underhanded, evil, sneaky, and corrupt behavior.

If this kind of behavior isn't corrected at an early age, then the genetic pool or the DNA of parents, can put us all in the same boat. According to Proverbs 22:6, *"Train up a child in the way he should go and when he is old he will not depart from it,"* (KJV). It says, "Train them in the way they should go." It didn't say let them go the way they want to go. Unfortunately, that is what's happening in many cases, constituting such a wicked society. An attitude of that

> "Train up a child in the way he should go and when he is old he will not depart from it" (Proverbs 22:6 KJV).

magnitude creates a wicked disposition in their lives and a beautiful relationship with no one. Sad to say, but you may not reap where you sow, but you will reap what you sow.

Building up the Relationship

Now, we all know that relationships must be worked on and built up to reach some happy goals. Would you agree that goals are no more important than the person? Your goals are no more important than your ability to reach them.

I use the terms 'worked on,' and 'built up.' Think of your relationship as a building or a house. Would you want a *shack relationship* or would you prefer a *mansion relationship*? Not the shack, I hope. This would mean always arguing and refuting dispositions or principles, no gas in the car, no food in the refrigerator, and children out of control because the parents are out of control. The children becoming the product of their environment and the vicissitudes of life always coming against them like a flood. Because of no moral restraints, there are more ups and downs than a 40-year-old elevator.

Now the mansion relationship is created when all the minor details of disagreements are handled in a civilized manner. Never let normalities of life become abnormalities. If it takes a rhetorical analysis and some quality time to work things out, then do so, even if you to have to isolate yourself from society for a while. Your mate should be your ultimate concern. Now, I hope you both can see yourself constantly rising to the top to live in the glorified atmosphere of God's very best. Amen! Are you understanding now the difference between the shack and the mansion relationship life?

The Bible says, *"What therefore God has joined together, let no man put asunder* (Matthew 19:6, KJV). In Hebrews 13:4, God says, *"Marriage is honorable among all and the bed undefiled,"* (KJV). The bed undefiled conveys the idea that the Lord approves of sexual intimacy between a husband and wife. This does not give any grounds to fornicators, adulterers, homosexuals, or lesbians. Their sins will have particularly damaging ramifications. As I stated earlier, I am not suggesting that a relationship is always over because of an argument, but use a little wisdom.

If that man can't stop busting up your face or if that woman can't seem to find her and her man's bed, then leave the devil and come live with us (just joking). Jesus invited us 2000 years ago. God made preparations 6000 years ago. Yes, He invited the hurting, the blind degenerates, and the ridiculously remarkable. Yeah, the high-saditty, sedated, quiet, iceberg type, lord of the Dukes aristocrats, and even the goofy, spooky, faithless, hopeless, misery laden, drastically disrupted, the politicians, Canadians, and the vegetarians all were invited. Amen!

Part of the intensity of love is vulnerability which involves giving all of yourself to your partner and being straight-up and honest. There is little reward if you both aren't honest and it creates a secrecy in the relationship.

Just months ago, you said you love her. Just months ago, you said you love him. Now, neither one of you will give the other the time of day from watch out of a German Cracker Jack box or two grains of Russian popcorn. Isn't this a crashing

Goodyear blimp? In 1960, there was a science fiction movie about a cryogenic expert.

Cryogenic- deals with subjects, it is the branch of physics dealing with product production and effects of very low temperature.

When he died, his wife, who was an abuser, demanded that his body be frozen. Afterwards, an icy apparition was haunting her, calling her to join him in a frosty grave. I said to myself, *"Well, I'll be a Southern Mississippi smutty, midnight   crow-black, mud-sucking, Belgium cattle dog; I know he didn't!"*

Apparition: a ghost or ghostlike image of a person.

Could this happen in your abusive relationship? Will you be taking hot chocolate or ice cream to that frosty grave? What's so ironic is, in many of these cases, these kinds of people will fight over that significant other until he or she is in the grave. This icy apparition (ghost) was nothing more than a 'so-called' supernatural frosty icy apparition of her man. How romantic! In an abusive relationship, it may at times seem awfully romantic- fighting over a loved one. It certainly is a natural instinct, but beyond this inceptive impulse and the honor to undo your ego, it really doesn't make any sense.

Love is most likely to work when both individuals (the affluent or influential, moral or immoral, regenerated or degenerated) are loving each other with equal intensity. That also includes obligations and commitment. The Bible says, [12]*"For we dare not make ourselves of the number, or compare ourselves with those that commend themselves; but they are measuring themselves, by themselves and comparing themselves among themselves are not wise.* [18] *For not he that commend of himself is approved, but whom the Lord commendeth* (2 Corinthians 10:12, 18, KJV). So, the couple next door may be doing something in their marriage that wouldn't work in your marriage. The reason there aren't any perfect marriages or anything else, is simple. It's because there aren't any perfect people. I promise you, your marriage will not work if you think it's because she is pretty. Please don't marry her only because she is pretty or because he is handsome. I hear it all the time, "Man, she sure is pretty!" For what it is used for, a baseball glove is pretty.

Ma Burker and Bonnie Parker were also pretty, but they were two of the evilest women that has ever lived. They would take their machine guns and turn bodies into hamburger. Beauty on the outside does not always mean beauty on the inside, not by a long shot. You may have met some women at the bar doing the 5 o'clock happy hour. Did it ever occur to you that most people at the happy hour are looking for happiness? Understand this, very few people are happy when they get there and many has defamed sugar by the time they leave. There is so much that the public does not see of a person's private/ inner character.

You might know how much a person drinks in public, but have no idea how much they drink in private. If you keep allowing these people to dictate your direction, I promise you that you are headed for the agony of defeat. You may be getting information from someone today, who may be headed for the nut-house tomorrow. The one who's counseling you today, tried to drown a fish yesterday. That's why I say, "Study the casual relationships first." You've heard it said, "Oh, he sure is handsome." Yeah, on the outside, but he has just been released from the inside of prison for killing his wife and another woman for insurance money.

The real reason the defense said, he just lost it-temporarily insanity, was because of a few technicalities. Now he is home free and looking for his next wife or victim to be. These are the kind of people you should be cautious of, especially women. Let me explain!

Most people usually go into a relationship expecting permanence, especially women. In many cases, the tire slashing, window busting, and poison feeding people are women. It is because many men have awakened the beast in them and in some cases, with their help. Why let him in your bosom when you knew he was a snake from the beginning? However, you have to study him first to know he's a snake.

You see ladies, love is an explosive, expressive commodity of the heart, not the head. Why didn't you rent him an apartment in your head before building him a mansion in your heart, only to be foreclosed on after all of your investment? He has probably discovered gifts in you that he doesn't have himself, and that is not only your ability to survive, but to take care of him while doing so.

Surviving is really a gift. Surviving means continuing to live or exist especially in spite of danger or hardship. Could that be the reason for this one-sided/secret relationship? Taking care of him because of your precious gift. Ok men! I know this is not a one-way thing. I have also been victimized.

My point is, people take advantage of each

other. Don't allow your gift to take you where your character cannot keep you. You may end up with anything from petty theft to a murder charge after finding out just how much you have been used. Love is only exalted by the imagination of two people agreeing with the same goals in mind. God gives us gifts, but He tells us to "*Be ye transformed by the renewing of our minds*" (Romans 12:2, KJV). He did not say, "Be ye gifted," but "Be ye transformed."

Transformation is the ultimate break for elevation. Just like Satan will not hang out where there is holiness and roaches will not hang out where there is bug spray, nor will your lazy significant other hang out where there is work required.

Establishing a Foundation

Don't claim to have been misdirected when you failed to establish the laws of your own domain. Any so-called significant other, constantly sending out mixed signals with little to no romantic sense of significance, should be kicked to the curb. They're just another bye-gone apparition, conducive to nothingness or the paragon of never was, but could have been. Don't just fall for anybody. Only God Himself can replicate or rehash such a paragon just for you. Now, I'm not suggesting that you're lonely just because you are or may be alone. However, some people are alone and lonely, feeling down and under. You may be the underdog, underpaid, underprivileged, and maybe even misunderstood, but it's only another position to overcome. Now, as I stated earlier in many ways, don't just keep rushing into relationships without some serious

> **Apparition**: a ghost or ghostlike image of a person.

observations. Don't expect it to be normal and right, when it started out ever so wrong. If you see any flags at all, notice if there are any red ones. If so, get out quick. It doesn't take a genius to spot it, if you are cautious. If the relationship is good and there are any flags at all, there will not be a red one. I've been around just a little while and I know some educational true stories. If your relationship is down and under, then there is only one direction to travel, and that's 'up.'

Some of these relationships (past, present, and possibly future) are tastefully delightful or could be referred to as delectable. On the other hand, there are those whom I know of who has been and some still are distastefully disgusting or repulsive. I have said on numerous occasions, "You can't beat two people working together," but I meant working together with each other and not against each other.

Concentration-camp Relationship

Perspicuous: (of an account or representation) clearly expressed and easily understood; lucid

While there is still time and a lot more life to live, get out of that concentration-camp relationship. Sweet living is as perspicuous as the nose on your face, (whenever you decide to take a look at it). I'm talking about plain to the understanding, especially because of clarity and precision of presentation.

Get out of those no-good relationships, whoever you are. Life is too short for a lot of sorrow. Will you be happy tomorrow? You could be. You'll never know the jewel God has for you until you are free of the one you are with, who seems demon inspired. He or she may be the one that you are best without. When will you realize that you deserve better? When will you stop thinking that the mistake will correct itself? No, it won't; you correct it. Until you learn to let go, you'll never realize that your out-go may position you for your true income. The right in-come could be the right person, the happiness, the money, and all of life's benefits, not a crushed face as I mentioned earlier.

Hey! Let me tell you this, there was a time when I was so intimidated that if confidence was a bomb, the blast wouldn't have ruffled the filaments in a bowl of cotton. There are so many like that today, with fear of what others might think, putting themselves in vulnerable positions and trying to please everybody.

How do you stand behind a relationship that you're not working on yourself? You could be the problem. You may even be the reason things are going, if not gone, sour. Then we ask God to bless this mess. Without God, we cannot; without us, He will not. We must work together. We must participate. It shouldn't be God doing it all.

How can you call a one-sided relationship a perfect match? It's a mess, not a match and without a match you don't get a spark, much less a fire.

Togetherness is what make it so great; whereas, selfishness is what make the relationship so stupid.

When a man is flirting vertically, only to succeed horizontally, don't be foolish enough to think that's romance. He is only looking for a chance to enhance the thrill of getting in your pants. In fact, one part of the definition of horizontal is "As a person lying down," but many will go on through with the booty call, fulfilling the expectations of the other partners at the moment. It's the hopes that it will be beneficial for the relationship later, only to encounter the inevitable, disappointment of it not coming to fruition. If a relationship is not all about the both of you and is only all about just one of you, then it is technically a long lustful date that will end as soon as either one of you has had enough. Wonder how I know what I'm talking about? This is another one of the educational truths I'm being honest with you about.

Honesty is the pre-condition or pre-requisite of a golden relationship. Therefore, if you start with secrets, you have really started out with the intentions of deception. Now, there is the possibility of starting a relationship for a positive and beautiful surprise later; I understand that. Let's make sure that if there are any secrets, it is for that reason only.

Now, a house with an angry, lazy, and especially broke woman is uninhabitable. It can leave you, not only mentally, but magically twisted. *Abraca-slap* her, just a little word play, that's all (no slapping allowed).

On another occasion, a woman said, "I'm here to meet my husband's needs, but I just can't follow his lead. I just can't trust my husband's decision. Well, being the tyrant that she was, I could understand why. I wouldn't follow his lead either; look who he married. People in prison wouldn't follow anyone's lead and people in mental institution couldn't follow anyone's lead. God gave us a head for thinking and a tail to sit on. Heads we win; tails we lose. You'll never possess what you do not pursue (not honestly).

Someone once said, "If you are pursuing long life, get a pet." Some people say pet owners live longer. Well, if the size of the pet has anything to do with life longevity, I think I'll buy an elephant. You know, I say this in reference to wasted money of the past, there has been too many years of my youth left behind without one good thought beyond yesterday. Looking for those years, I couldn't find one in the daytime with a flashlight. It's as stupid as being blind-folded, looking for something in the dark, trying to see the invisible, or touching the intangible.

If I had it to do all over again, I promise you that there would be a lot more "NOs" than "YESES" and that's for sure. Well, I can't do like *Tyrone Davis* and 'Turn back the hands of time," so I am believing God to make my latter years my better years. Amen!

Rebirth- Renewed Relationship

The Bible is a doctrine without error or faults in all its teachings, not the anti-biblical assumptions of man. So according to the Word of God, being born again is like new babies in the spiritual maternity ward. Little babies born without a past.

When you and your significant other gives birth to a new relationship, it is not completely without a past. Either of you can bring some issues in, simply because it is the death of an old relationship and the birth of a new one. Now that should require very little thought-to-thought combat. Yeah! The new relationship cannot come, in most cases, without a past, but it should never start out with a lot of negative insight in human behavior. Rhetoric can tear a relationship from top to bottom, causing devastating mental-combat, if you allow it. These relationships are usually short lived, lasting about as long as a snowball in the fiery furnaces. The relationship is misfiring like bad spark plugs. Get out! If you will, quickly realize the inadequacies of a crumbling relationship. You will have to conclude that you are on an impossible mission.

Think about it!

Are you involved with someone intimately, other than your spouse or are you the victim? If so, then why keep hanging onto a dehydrated relationship? Is it social economical dependency or just so much love that you just can't let go? If you don't do something about the infidelity and the heartbreaking cheating, then you are cheating. You're cheating yourself.

The relationship should reach its apex at some point if either one of you are thinking longevity. Marriage is a bilateral commitment with reciprocal rights and duties. In many cases, the warehouse of one person's kind personality will not complete the inventory of the other mate's needs, not to mention wants. In other words, you cannot buy your way into all relationships. That has been my problem in years past.

Now, if you are financially able and that is the agreement, then God is in agreement as long as you keep Him- God first. Amen! Don't go into that relationship with one-sided thinking, not ever having learned to give as much as you receive. Mutual respect in a relationship plays a big part in the relationship's longevity and the happiness that both of you experience. A man always feels emasculated when his wife or girlfriend believes or even act as if he is not good enough.

Eugene Barnes

The Ego Battle

Ego plays a big part in relationships too. When a woman loses an ego battle, she feels controlled and restricted. When a man loses an ego battle, he feels emasculated. Oh, and about this salary, a guy subconsciously feels like the hunter and the provider in the relationship.

> **Emasculated**: to deprive of strength, vigor, or spirit: WEAKEN

Scoffing at the one thing in his role, which is earning for the family, would definitely make him feel like he's less of a man. Ladies, don't call your man a coward just because he wouldn't confront someone or deal with a situation. Instead, reason and converse with him about what the better action could have been, while empathizing with him at the same time. No guy likes being compared negatively to another guy, especially by his own girlfriend or wife. Always talk about any flaws either one of you may have privately. Never confront each other in front of friends, his or yours.

Never say to each other, "I knew you wouldn't be able to do it." Hearing this from a woman he loves, feels like a painfully low blow to the crotch. What's worse is, he can't even argue his case simply because he has failed in your eyes. It's as if you are simply adding to what he already knows. Don't ever shatter a man's myth by turning it into a reality, for then he'll need another woman and a drink of liquid courage.

Now men, don't make fun of your wife if she wakes up with a cracked-up face because she failed to remove her make-up. If that happens Ms., then don't let your emotions overwhelm your tolerance, capacity, or your ability to control yourself. Many selfish, egotistical people will never admit how miserable life can be without a loving mate. I have sung these same old songs myself, as well as anyone else. Songs like, '*When I get home, I don't have to hear any lip from nobody.*' Things like, '*No matter how long I'm gone; my dog is always glad to see me.*' Now, I'm not suggesting that you are lonely because you're alone, as I stated earlier, but if you desire a companion, then you need to be married, not shacking up. If you think I'm joking about the shacking up, then remember God will judge and He won't be joking. Nothing escapes God's attention; therefore, nothing will escape His judgment. Just because God is not loud, doesn't mean He isn't serious. Again! God is not the least bit affected or controlled by creation or creaturehood. So, God's way is marriage before sex, like it or not. If you love someone, I mean really love them, then you should know that love isn't some temporary mental and intellectual exercise before sex. It is imperative that you know this.

All people has some mental imperfection. Does that mean that no one is perfect? Absolutely! The abnormalities and non-consistencies of life have many traumatic challenges and we must prepare for them. It is the preparation for these challenges that will and has helped some people to stand mentally strong in adverse circumstances.

Don't battle with it until you are mentally cracked before doing so.

Leave! Please leave papa, leave mama and save yourself from unnecessary drama. That is the normative for choleric relationship freedom. Unnecessary: meaning not needed.

> **Choleric:** extremely irritable or easily angered; irascible

Choleric: meaning *bad tempered and irritable. It's cantankerous and argumentative behavior*. Stop trying to convince someone that they should love you when you already know what you see.

Stop calling that bear a bull and don't call that Lions a Fox. Giraffes and Leopards have spots. Cheetahs and Dalmatians have spots. Birds and Bumblebees fly. I'm sure you can differentiate the species. Although they are all animals, they are not the same, any more than a good relationship when one is loving and the mate is not.

Do you know what, 'I need my space,' means? It means, "I'm making myself intentionally unavailable; I'm fed up, or I've had enough." If the person needing space doesn't have anyone else at the moment, then *I need my space* really means, "I don't want you." Yeah, in that so-called nice way, it is, "I need my space." Well, as far as I'm concerned, you can have all the space you want, as long as I don't have to go into space with you. (Height is not a hobby of mine to climb). Speaking from a vertical perspective.

Horizontally, if you make it to the other side of the earth, you're much too close. From my astronomical studies, your vertical departure would be far more exciting. There is far-far more room vertically than horizontally. If you can hear and understand the words, "It is over," then a stroboscopic dismissal should be greatly appreciated. The relationship will never reach its apex-climax. A stroboscopic dismissal is leaving in a flash, and one of you should quickly conclude it to be necessary if the other hasn't already done so. No one is forcing you to be intractable. It leads to uncontrollable difficulties causing one or the other, in most cases to be un-accommodating, inflexible, unyielding, pig-headed, and rigid. You may be hurt, but that does not justify violence. Don't let your emotions to overwhelm your capacity or ability to control yourself. Remember, you're sending your relationship into space. I know you've heard them say, "Well, he's my baby daddy!" Or, "She is my baby mama!"

S- Stay
H-Help
I-Inspire
P-Protect

Everybody you've ever seen has or has had a mama and daddy. You know, my heart really goes out to the hurting, but the choleric and acerbic barbarians, I just can't sympathize with. You know that 'my baby daddy' is an excuse! What kind of father is he? What kind of mother is she? Really! Is she a mother because she never took the time to crawl inside of her baby daddy's head before crawling into his bed? Why don't you try developing yourself into a real lady and that will qualify you to demand a real gentleman?

Remember this before you embark upon your next relationship. A boy or a so-called man will come and go, but a real gentleman will come in on a S.H.I.P. Yes! Boys and so-called men will come and go, but a genuine gentleman is there to capitalize the 'M' in man.

Someone once said, "If a gentleman leaves you, he will leave you speechless; when he let go, he will let go of his pride and continue to pursue you by keeping the dust off your relationship. A real gentleman will wait until you are married to lie: to lie down with you. A real gentleman will make and keep all the women jealous of his woman before he makes his woman jealous of other women, simply because you are a well taking care of lady. A gentleman will attract the attention of many, but only has eyes for his lady. If you have a man who cheats, then you have a clandestine recalcitrant that has not obligated himself to marital faithfulness. What's in him was there all along; it was just a matter of time before the withdrawal.

Recalcitrant- resisting authority or control; not obedient or compliant; refractory. -Hard to deal with, manage, or operate.

I see banks almost everywhere I travel and so do you, but you are only limited to withdraw where you have made deposits. You will withdraw from the bank of larceny, if you are a thief. If you are a talebearer, you will withdraw from the bank of gossip. If you cheat, you will withdraw from your adultery or fornication account. If you drink, then you may get a good old shot of that liquid courage, which makes you feel a lot less guilty.

New Relationships

Well, it's about time that I tell you more about my new relationship. Now, she is not new in my life in terms of familiarity because I've know her since I was about nine years old. However, I lost contact with her after she graduated from high school, (four years before me). Now, around the age 34, my path crossed with her again only for another heartbreak. We were both married at that time. I knew the man she married. We all were schoolmates, but at that time, she knew me not. However, I was thrilled to know that she hadn't left the state of North Carolina. Little did I know, patience of chronology would someday take its toll. It paid off.

You see, fifty-five years ago, I fell madly in love with her at age nine. She was back in my life to stay after my divorce and the death of her husband. She came into my life as a woman of

God. A God-fearing woman, an absolute paragon. I had said so many times, in times gone by that, "It takes a certain quality of character to be called a lady and a certain quality of character to be called a gentleman." There are many males and females and many men and women who do not fall or fit in the category of *ladies* and *gentlemen*. Ladies and gentlemen are the acknowledgement of the noble. It describes those who are highly elevated in character and impressive in appearance. Dukes, Earls, Princesses, Kings, and Queens, although many of these elite aristocrats were not so noble in character, but one could not deny their authority and ability to rule and reign.

In a good relationship, a gentleman will pursue her disparately until she is his wife and cherishes her long after the marriage celebration. A gentleman will keep the dust out of their relationship. He will bless her with unexpected gifts from time-to-time, without it always been some special occasion.

That's right! After the anniversary, after Christmas, after her birthday, for she is still his wife or significant other. She is still to be respected at all times. With sweet inspirations, there just ain't no telling what a satisfied woman might do. She may keep on living and keep on giving your way.

Now! May I further enlighten you on my wife to-be? We have both had our ups and downs in other relationships. We have had more ups and downs then the greatest of elevator services and we can't undo anything, good or bad. We are doing everything in our God-given ability to do the things which are pleasing in God's sight. There is an affinity between Betty and I. My fiancée and I came into an agreement when we concluded that time is a major factor in bringing a relationship from casual to the magnificent

> **Affinity-** spontaneous or natural liking or sympathy for someone or something. - a similarity of characteristics suggesting a relationship

manifestation of marvelous. We have both seen many, many times when we were out enjoying the day of life and noticed how other couples carried on. Some couples seemed to be so casual, not that we were expecting to see much PDA, (public display of affection).

Now, I don't want you to think that I am the only one working on gentlemen's quality, but I have not seen one out of the last fifty couples, of which the man opened the car door for his woman. I know it is impossible for me to see everything and I'm not suggesting that it isn't happening. However, could it be the reason why so many relationships go sour? Yeah! We have seen couples going in and out of grocery stores, shopping malls, businesses, and especially churches, and the man did not open the door for his spouse/significant other. This is not means of acidulous or sub-acid criticism, just an observation. That's just one of many things and many reasons why sweet inspiration is lacking. Women have told me, "That's alright, I can open the door for myself," and I said, "I wasn't suggesting that your physically ability was diminishing, but I am totally perplexed as to whether you are so far from being a lady, that you can't recognize a gentleman. I believe you can open the door for yourself and if you are ever on my car again, you surely will and until you learn to act like a lady, you have grossly disqualified yourself as a lady, woman," (Just kidding). I will make the offer again, that's my nature. Now concerning my future wife, Sister Betty Lou, if we were into Greek or Roman mythology, Betty would be my Leto, my sweet little Leto. Leto

> **Acidulous**: somewhat acid or harsh in taste or manner

was a goddess. She was a Greek Latin goddess of motherhood. Zeus, who was Leto's husband, married another woman named Hera, while Leto was pregnant. Leto was pregnant before the marriage with Hera, but she was still jealous of Leto. Did I mention that Leto was pregnant with twins (Apollo and Artemis)? Zeus vetoed everybody's plan of action and refusal against Mrs. Leto. My point refers to what I mentioned earlier about a gentleman making other women jealous of his woman. My Betty is most amative, an inclination towards love, and not amatory. Do not confuse these words. This is not a character blemish, if we are understanding here. She is so huggable; I can't see her not being so lovable.

She is incomparable and without equal in quality- matchless, unparalleled, peerless and unmatched. She is irreplaceable, inspirational, and almost immortal. Being totally mesmerized, I thought I was in paradise. She is my provocative, passionate, pride and joy.

Amatory- of, causing, or showing love. **Amative-** of or inclined to love

She is a quick witted, radiant, remarkably ravishing, and magnificently dazzling queen. What makes her so unique and unforgettable is her unselfishness, understanding, and undemanding heart. Yeah! She came into my life fifty-years ago, but at that time the relationship was only a fantasy that has now become a reality.

Lethologica is the precise word for not being able to recall the precise word and I can't recall the precise words to express my feelings precisely. A relationship that is open to good communication is like furniture polish for the furniture. Do you know that sitting a can of furniture polish on the furniture will not keep it from getting dusty? It must be used to get some shine. If not, it will become as dull with dust as a foggy night; there will be no vision whatsoever. Why can't we create an atmosphere conducive to goodness, if not greatness? If you treat each other good long enough, it may turn out to be something great.

Hey ladies, if you want to be treated like a lady, please search out the qualities of a gentleman. You should have done that already, but I understand baby girl, if you hadn't been taught. Teaching is an impartation of knowledge from the teacher's head to the student, from the mentor's head to the protégé or apprentice. Make sure you search for a qualified instructor as well, most definitely with a biblical conception of the sweet and wonderful facilitating life. If you take any other route for good sweet, Godly living, it would be absolutely unreasonable.

Remember, although I said to search out some gentleman qualities, the Bible still says, *"Whosoever find a wife, finds a good thing, and obtains favor of the Lord"* (KJV). The living Bible says, *"The man who finds a wife finds a good thing, and she is a blessing to him from the Lord* (Proverbs 18:22). So, I'm only suggesting that you search out or search for gentleman qualities and not him. You do that as they pursue you. Amen! Amen!

The Bible is an ongoing process that's constantly giving rest to your spirit. If you can receive that part of this message, I believe you will find your life far more rewarding. This is not an obligation or a prohibition that has been impose on you. The Bible says in Psalm 46:10, *"Be still and know that I am God; I will be exalted among the heathen, I will be exalted in the earth,"* (KJV). So be cool young lady, be cool young man; just because God isn't loud, doesn't mean He has refused to see you through. Amen!

I'll say this again and again, don't ever try convincing someone that they should love you. If the love isn't there, no special event and not even the President, no storm, no amount of money, nor a single episode of anything can make it happen.

Propinquity: the state of being close to someone or something; proximity

No! Money can't buy love, but you can bet it can buy what you like to do. That's only momentary pleasure. So, ladies when that right man comes along, and men when the right lady comes along, I promise that geographical propinquity will show you favor. That place of location will be highly beneficial to the both of you for years to come. Location can be the key to your success if you will allow God to direct your steps and dictate your directions. Now, this is one way to tell if you're in the wrong place. You are in the wrong place when you're in the wrong face-showing too much emotion into the absolute merciless, caustic, and heartless. Don't even play in the snow with them. You may be feeling the effects of a rock-loaded snow-ball at any given moment. They can make your life so miserable and jejune.

The sadness, regret, and distress can insidiously take its toll on your mind then your body. I wouldn't be afraid to predict that at least ninety percent (90%) of the cold heartedness is because they are broken-hearted. Yep! We may think they are cold, when the real issue is, they are

Insidiously: in a gradual, subtle way, but with harmful

only sad. Remember, this does not nullify the fact, whether coldhearted or broken-hearted, that your garbage should not, and I repeat, should not be taken into your next relationship.

From Ex to Next

Don't even think about moving onto the next, until you have overcome your ex. No one wants to smell your exe's poop, but you. Don't be so stupid to do such a thing. It is an incredible display of your ignorance and stupidity. Someone once said, 'God created people to be loved and things to be used.' In this chaotic loving world, it's just the opposite. Loving things and using people is a switched-off brain decision. You see pain, tears, and heartbreak should make you stronger, braver, and wiser. Now remember I mentioned 'wiser.' So, please give thanks to God for your educational past darkness which should have made you wiser.

Your future now has a much more marvelous and brighter light. I speak these words, not from my heart only, but from experience. Better to have a heart without words, then words without heart. I'm so glad I'm not heartless; I just learned to use my heart less. Insidious, enticing, and petulant in your life is much like mental poisoning that is usually detected much too late. How many times will the same old foolish things keep happening until we finally get it? Will it be weeks? Will it be months? Will it be years? Some of us will never get it. There are many people today, at a well-seasoned age, still living and looking smart while making dumb decisions. That's right. A seasoned age, but not the least bit of salt or pepper in their decisions.

I was inspired and almost obsessed with foolish and unreasoning passion when I met Betty years ago. I really don't think it would have been a wise idea, for her to let me catch her if she had known me back then. Those years were a fantasy, as I stated earlier. I was a very, very foolish man when it came to women, from a financial and emotional perspective.

Today, Betty and I are both much wiser. She has filled with wisdom as she aged. She has truly defined the laws of aging, by aging so slowly and gracefully and that is another thing that makes her so unique. She has added a lot of muscle to my emotional constitution and has added a lot of zeal to the Eugene Barnes administration.

Before I met Betty, or crossed paths with her again, I had not realized that being so anti-traditionalist was so much fun.

Idiosyncratic: relating to idiosyncrasy; peculiar or individual.

Again, the 'monkey see, monkey do' standard of living is not anything we play. We don't believe in or contemplate on what other people say. Idiosyncratic is something too peculiar to encounter and we are a peculiar people. We are peculiar, atypical, and deviant. The best minds are idiosyncratic. No, Betty and I will never attempt that monkey see, monkey do mimicry. If we don't see what other monkey see, we are a lot less likely to do what other monkeys do. It is a mimicry with limited knowledge and concern of the consequences. If it is an idiomatic expression, it's either the meaning changing or it's meaningless. Your relationship does not have to be this way. It only happens if you allow it; saying that this way of living is 'okay' and I'll do whatever you want me to do, no matter how stupid. It is not the least bit etiquette. No sense of dignity. No chance of proving that you are a person of sound mind. Now, etiquette is a code of behavior that delineates expectations for social behavior according to contemporary conventional norms within a society, social class, or a group.

> **Mimicry:** the action or art of imitating someone or something, typically in order to entertain or ridicule.

Yes, my Betty and I will remain idiosyncratic and unpredictable; following the course of life's unfathomable future and unknown

> **Unfathomable-** incapable of being fully explored or understood.

discoveries. Totally oblivious to God's divine plan.

Significant Other

Periodically, I must allude to my fiancé because I must be first partaker of the fruit. It is my intentions to help establish some gentleman quality thinking, because too much casual living in a relationship can lead to too many causal disappointments and is eventually great contributions for failure.

Now, my significant other is my Queen, simply because I am her King. I am not always right by a long shot, but I do have the right to make my own decisions, and I have decided to make her my Queen. I told her on one occasion that she was almost, as I see her, immortal. It is a never dying, never decaying, never ending, and never ceasing love. I will protect it so it will last forever. It is my responsibility to mitigate or annihilate, obliterate, and to utterly destroy any antagonizing things that crosses her path. I will strongly disapprove of any outrageous behavior or tomfoolery.

I really enjoy making her happy, and not by making promises to her that I don't intend to keep. I love making her laugh, especially in a throw-your head back, uncontrollable manner. I will never take her from laughter to tears. That is not my intentions.

As I mentioned, she has aged so slowly and matured so gracefully which is another thing that makes her so unique. Ladies, if your relationship is a high maintenance one that is causing problems, get off your high horse and try being a little more understanding, rather than intentionally misunderstood.

> **Deleterious:** harmful often in a subtle or unexpected way

For example, let's talk about money.

Money issues has been deleterious, detrimental, and extremely damaging to many relationships. It has been more adverse and inimical, causes than infidelity. Statistics has shown approximately 89 to 90% over infidelity. Many men and women have gone into relationships financially clandestine (with a future that is financially deceptive). Yep, they're coming into your life with high hopes of what you can do for them. After thirty-eight (38) long years of drown out marriage between two women, I have seen more inspirational love in the two eyes of Betty in four months, than I saw in the four eyes of my two exes in thirty-eight years. Now that is not a putdown, but a critical observation. We are all still friends, but at one time in our life we were immature.

When you meet that right person; *Mr. or Ms. Whoever* he or she is, it will be like serendipity happenstance- that unsought, unintended, or unexpected pleasant surprise. I already know that my fiancé prefers freedom rather than bondage. That's what we want, that's what we'll have. I know opposition is ineluctable, inevitable, inescapable, but understand this, don't wait until it arrives. Educate yourself; be prepared. It's as easily done, as said. It's the same as making up your mind to be mature. I chose to be mature and not be so far from the reality of being a gentleman, that I can't recognize a real lady. It will help you to learn to appreciate and hold onto the one you have. It will teach you to be ready when the right one comes along, ladies and gentlemen.

There was a time when I lived in the hot and sweaty grips of fear that another economical dependent female would walk into my life again, only to be asked to walk right back out. You see, there are so many different personalities, you can't put everyone in the same category. I'm free of that fear. Betty and I have chosen to live the utopia lifestyle. That's right! The utopia way of living. Don't you dare sit around and wait for someone to make you happy. You must choose to do so before that special person comes along. They are more likely to take an interest in you. So, wash up your body, get your hair fixed, get a haircut, get your nails done, buy you some new clothes, if you can afford to (if not, clean up the ones you have). If you drink at least once a week or do drugs, you can afford some new clothes. Ask me how I know. So many times, we say we can't afford to do the things that we need to do, but anything that is just flat out stupid can always seem to come to pass or is accomplished.

Now, if anyone ever tell you that you are no good, that is all the more reason to prove them wrong. That is reason enough to make sure they see just who you can be. Life can be so facilitating when you are with the one you really love and not just some sex object. Stay away from those acidulous, acrimonious, sarcastic, and debatable barbarians. They are not the least bit concerned about your welfare. The only four-fold world power of defense for survival is Social Services, Medicaid,

> **Acrimonious**: (typically, of speech or a debate) angry and bitter.

food stamps, and oatmeal. Just as broke as a 1548 slave, just as broke as a 13th century share-cropper, I'm talking about these broke arrogant attitudes. Many of them talking about who they don't like or who they can't stand. They shouldn't be able to stand to see anyone walk by without lending a helping hand, hand me downs, grits, and stolen butter. Now, I'm not making fun of anything, but the nasty attitudes, wayward, insubordinate, undisciplined, and recalcitrant. What a shame! Now, these are some of those that are cunning enough to lure you into a relationship. You must be on the lookout. Watch it! You could find yourself in another relationship just as contingent, possibly unforeseeable, and even unpredictable as your last relationship. I believe that my relationship, or our relationship is God and Heaven ordained.

For Betty's sake, I hope that after we are married, kisses don't become snowflakes. She may find herself in one of my most severe snowstorms with my very strong and high winds, and for her, very low visibility. The super love or the love to come is inexorable, inescapable, unavoidable, and by all means, unprecedented. The ground-breaking, revolutionary kind of love, epoch-making which means a particular time or an event in a person's life. I intend for our wedding and honeymoon to be one marked by notable events and screenplay like

Hollywood have never heard. I'm just trying to give you a little insight about the overpowering influence of the love between a man and a woman unalterable and undiluted love. I believe our love complements each other perfectly because marital love, properly perceived and practiced, is the strongest human bond. For it is not only a physical union of the bodies, but also a spiritual communion of personalities. Because of the limitless love and supernatural possibilities of God, I believe we will override and overrule the quarrelsome, the fractious, the irritable, and the disgruntled. Anything in that category must sit down, for it was defeated at the cross. My Lord and Majestic Savior saw to that. Yes, He did, at the cross when He hung His head and said, "It is finished." It is imperative that you know this. There is nothing supraliminal concerning this, nothing occurring without awareness.

Nothing above the threshold of perception; nothing to render you beyond your ability to make a sound decision, you and your significant other should make it your number one priority to annihilate tomfoolery, and the tommyrot. Not mitigate or decimate, but obliterate, annihilate, and to completely put out of existence.

My knowledge of a kingdom is, there is no kingdom without a constitution. I will constitute and enforce the laws of my kingdom and protect my Queen. The constitution in a kingdom constitutes the expressed will of the King. It is not '**a**' but '**the**' royal contract and documented will, purposes, and intentions of the King.

A Kingdom's constitution is stamped with the essence of the nature, character, and personality of the King. A contract generated by the people is a democracy; it's the complete opposite of a kingdom. Because you 'O King' is the one responsible for the originated and complete rules of your kingdom, exclusively from your heart and mind, the citizens or the people of your kingdom family, friends, commanders,

Eugene Barnes

| Tyrannical-characteristic of tyranny; oppressive and controlling. | or anybody that can likely cause a problem in you and your spouse relationship, should have no input concerning the |

terms or the conditions of your household

Constitution. If you allow it, you have allowed

them to rewrite your constitutional household rules.

Now, you wouldn't want to look that manly

incomplete, would you? Your love contract is now

completely violated. A tyrannical regime is on the

rise to being established in your household at any

given moment after detecting your weakness. How

sad! Stupid, but sad.

By all means, I'm not here to execute, but

advocate. Most of us understand execution, at least

from the guilty perspective or in the criminal arena.

To advocate is the formal speech, such as by an

attorney after the trial is over, directed to the ladies

and gentlemen of the jury. To advocate, which is

the formal speech made to the court by the

defendant who has been found guilty prior to being

sentenced. This is part of the criminal procedure in some common law jurisdiction.

Again! My intention is to remind you to take control, but don't take control of each other. You two should take control of your relationship. I'm talking about some educational truths. I use the term educational truths because so much of this, I have experienced and not just heard. So much of this, I have seen right around me in this geographical location.

There was a case I knew of extremely well in which a woman had two children by two different men. As soon as the children were born, these splenetic, vitriolic, cantankerous, longtime economical dependent's fathers was gone. Not one single day did she ever receive one single American penny for child support from either of the child's biological father (as in so many cases). However, she married a man when the two children were very small, but at some point, they divorced. Believe it or not, she later married one of her children's pappy. The children were very, very grown by that time. It was for him, (her now new dependent) easy living. Well, as life goes on, we will encounter many issues that doesn't make sense, but we have to admit that much of it, we do understand. I know I do, because many of these relationships shine so bright in the threshold of perception.

There was a time when I made a bitter statement *like building my own franchise of women by using a very specific method to build and cultivate my audience.* I was going to use an extraordinary infrastructure of interconnected, interracial women of the elite social circle and not the social service dependents, like I had dealt with in times past. They would be my confidants, altered egos, chums, and cohorts. That would make them fluent in a particular task and rooted in idealism and service because of being so idealistic. I'm talking about a group of female philosophers which asserts that reality is mentally constructed or otherwise immaterial. A dynamic achievement because when you're idealistic, you dream of perfection whether in yourself or other people. For example, you might have the idealistic goals of helping greater relationships come to fruition. The adjective idealistic describes someone whose plan or goal of helping others are lofty, grand, and possibly unrealistic.

At the particular time of my disgusting, distasteful, vomitus misery, and despair maybe it shouldn't have come to fruition at a time when I thought it should. But now, because of my new relationship, I see greater heights and I'm taking higher leaps and bounds. I'm talking about seeing your woman as one of the elite social circles and not social service. Ladies, you must see your man as your knight in shining armor. Remember, you must not search for him, just be ready when he comes on the scene. Prepare yourself ladies and prepare yourself with enthusiasm.

Vehemently, prepare yourself with zeal, zest, and gusto, because the quality of your preparation will determine the quality of your performance. The avidity, the extreme eagerness will determine if he has found his **good thing**.

Believe me! He would know if he has the woman for the Rib-eye steak relationship or the bologna and cheese sandwich relationship.

Are you optimistic for a great relationship or are you just waiting on some defeatist despondent, and pessimistic hook-up? Even if you're not faring so well, you don't have to look like you are on welfare, even if you are. What an incredible display of defeated failure. Don't sit around with a face looking as if it has been washed in lemon juice, you ate lemons for breakfast, and you drank lemon juice instead of milk or coffee. The drawing up of the face and the bitterness of the taste of life has left many women absolutely hopeless.

You must make that choice to take a chance or your life will never change. I have finally concluded that if you only fight to keep life at its norm; you will never experience the epitome of greatness. Listen! Hold your head up ladies.

Optimistic: hopeful and confident about the future.

Pessimistic: tending to see the worst aspect of things or believe that the worst will happen.

That mind-boggling knight in shining armor is on his way to turn your lonely world upside down. No, everybody that lives alone isn't always lonely, but when that one person who loves you for who you are comes along, I promise you that it will be incomprehensible infinitude, camaraderie will nullify all rhetoric; with an emotion that will punch like no professional fighter has ever done. Yeah! I am so proud to be writing this book at the time of the start of a new relationship. She is my Betty Lou and I can't say enough about her. I must empathize again the quality of life in this relationship and as a motivator; I must be first partaker of the fruit. Betty has proven to be that utopia of feminism and an impeccable paragon of peace. It takes a certain quality of character to function as a woman of God of that magnitude. She has chosen to do what any other woman of God can choose to do, and that is to

> **Indubitably:** impossible to doubt; unquestionable

move on through life with   indubitably, non-motivated dignity. If you have ever been motivated at all, stay motivated until you reach your goal.

Motivation is like jump-starting your car, getting a boost until you reach some place to buy another battery. Since this new relationship, we have had to do that. Don't turn your engine off until another battery is in view. No one should have to keep motivating you on the same issues. Because of the great qualities of mature ecstasy, Betty is self-motivated with unquestionable gladness.

The late great former Welterweight boxing champion Sugar Ray Robinson, once stated, "Real champions motivate themselves, and you have to believe in yourself when no one else will." The late great Kung Fu martial artist, Bruce Lee once stated, "I do not fear the man that practice 1000 kicks, but we must give all respect to the man that practice one kick a thousand times." Now, with that kind of focus for you as a couple, there isn't any chance of you two doing anything in life but winning. To function as a couple to the extreme pinnacle of greatness, you have to rise above the circumstances while facilitating in the glorified atmosphere of God's very best. Now that is awe-inspiring, breathtaking, and excellent sound wisdom.

"Thank you, Holy Spirit." Now let me apologize for the word impeccable and the way I used it earlier. Impeccable, meaning perfect?" No! Betty isn't perfect and no one else is. Guess I got a little carried away with factious tongue-in-cheek

> **Frolicsome:** lively and playful.

waggish jocular. There is nothing in that part that I allude to that is frolicsome by a long shot, but the Holy Spirit has proven Himself to be the infinite and supreme educator in our relationship and that He is the most infallible pedagogue, pedantic, and informal for our sake. Now that is domestic tranquility, with things running well in your house, if not in the country.

What really makes a relationship great is keeping other people and their advice-out. There is no love that has not been challenged. I've been in two particular relationships in times past that I cannot honestly say were a dream come true. If they were, please take me back to the dream and leave me there and there will be no remembrance of the realities. There will be no remembrance of the 'come true.'

Unfortunately for me, I have allowed myself to be controlled and dominated by the complexity and perplexities of life's circumstances, simply because of being so concerned about what other people thought. Being concerned about what people think does not constitute good relationships behavior, but a more accurate direction towards failure. Yeah! I had allowed myself to be juxtaposed or placed close together for a contrasting effect with others. Not necessarily to fit- in, but just wondering what their thoughts were concerning me. I did not spend my life in relationship dishonor or disrespect. I have been freed of the terrible miscarriages of relationship injustice. Your first relationship, after your father and mother should be God and then you should be taught to obtain the knowledge of God, Jesus Christ, and our keeper the Holy Spirit. I do not need your prestigious juxtaposition setting, just to fit in. I do not need to walk with the reputable, the distinguished, the celebrated, illustrious, or the renown. If I'm judged by anyone it is perfectly okay, as long as there isn't any serious defamation of my character or anything detrimental to my integrity.

Since Betty and I have been engaged, we have had one splenetic and acrimonious recalcitrant to desperately come against our relationship. Believe it or not, they say they are saved, born again, being redeemed by the blood of the Lamb. It almost makes you want to shed their blood. God forbid, smile y'all. Now, I have concluded on that issue that it is not my job to placate, appease, or pacify and hopefully, they will mature someday. It takes longer for some than for others. What make this issue anonymously bazaar (deviating from what is usual) is that this person wasn't an ex or a girlfriend and was married to someone else. She was as surprising as a snapper's bullet. You will never know what people will say about you because of what they think they know about you.

Extremely divergent, but I have learned not to retaliate. I am not the least bit vindictive. I didn't realize why she wasn't born in the seventeen or eighteen centuries until I had this startling revelation that she was born for a time such as this. I am here to help her while having a tolerance for this kind of behavior. I am a very well-controlled individual. It appears that she and many other people of that character suffers psychosomatically; which is nothing more than physical, outer sickness that starts from their mental factors: self-aggravated mental factors, such as internal conflict or stress, physical sickness, being the results of

> **Juxtaposition-** an act or instance of placing close together or side by side, especially for comparison or contrast

unforgiveness of self could she have been a 2,000year descendant of the Pharisees.

These irritable petulant are blatantly unconcealed and unashamed in the destruction of relationships. That is exactly what has been attempted in this case, but unfortunately for them it came not to fruition. Now, I'm almost convinced that these people like her and a few others who has come against this relationship are the Pharisees' descendants, because the last four letters in Pharisees could be shining the light on everything. The last four letters in *Pharisees* are s-e-e-s. They 'sees' everything you do. They 'sees' only the problem of others. They 'sees' only what is wrong in your case. They need to substantiate or corroborate their doctrine to prove that they are right.

Remember, there isn't a mosquito, tick, bug, lice, flea, fly, or gnat that has ever escaped God's attention, even during the nocturnal activities of the right. Now that really supercharged my faith in God's accurate judgment of His people. There is nothing in the dark that isn't there when the lights are on. No doubt, every writer is at sometimes a frustrated actor who recites his lines in the auditorium of his skull of his imagination. Maybe I'm only speaking for myself, but the limits of those lines are only those of the mind itself in the misty regions of your relationship.

She immediately became judgmental. I will not blindly follow the crowd or except their approach. I will not allow myself to indulge in the usual manipulating gerrymander to publicize a particular cause or point of view. I don't need to constitute relationship propaganda or relationship publicity, etc. Fortunately, for me I am brilliant; I am savvy enough to have transcended such nonsense. I have risen above that display of ignorance and stupidity. I have concluded that life is to be best lived and not conceptualized. I will no longer fall under the dictates of others. You better be mentally and verbally fine-tuned to precision when going into a new relationship. I can say I am happy because I am growing mentally daily and honestly not knowing where the limits lies. I want to be certain that every day is a new revelation, full of God given discoveries and possibilities. I cherish; yeah, I treasure, every memory of my downfalls and misfortunes, especially those that I was able to resolve. Sadly, many women act as if they didn't know that lust is a desire for their body, but love is a desire for their souls. The most spectacular, indescribable deep euphoric feeling for someone is Love.

Love and Lust

Love is a deep-seated feeling of emotions for someone that is barely comprehensible. True love isn't just a possession, but action. It is pleasing, enjoyable, pleasurable, satisfying, and delightfully hospitable. Love changes the oil, or the wheels of affection to keep a relationship on the go. Love is the service department of the beginning and the end of a relationship that last until death do us part.

The Bible says, "God is Love," not has loved, but is love. Love is His attribute not just a possession, (1 John 4:8). I have heard in times pass that 'You can give without loving, but you can't love, without giving.' Your brain will surely discern that loving touch, that beautiful smile, and the loving glare from his or her eyes will be processed almost immediately. This kind of love is a part of your life that you never want to get used to, or you may start taking it too casual and lose your emotional grips. I'm talking about the kind of love that makes your heart patter, smile, and blush when you see her, even if she hasn't done or said anything out of the ordinary. The love that truly excites you when she's around, but leaves you a little sad when she has to depart. Now that's before marriage, but you must keep it burning after the wedding, Amen! Amen!

There were times in my previous shacking, when our relationship was the most affable in public and at home pure cantankerous and barbaric. I wouldn't dare attempt to convince you that all the bright lights shown on me only. We were all young and foolish at times, all of us that had not been schooled on relationships, and that was most of us. I am so glad to be free of the exploiting games of role creation. I can honestly say that I'm not seeking some geographical setting on your stage to be schooled on relationships gerrymander, to create biased accusations, especially against hurting individuals.

This book isn't being written as some comical material; although, I may have been a little factious on some subjects, but a failing relationship can be so miserably devastating, lasting so long that most of your life it can be a long-lasting torment of hell, pure hell. In the beginning God created the heavens and the earth, but he did not create one problem or anything else to be problematic. Hey ladies, keep this in mind- that a man that findeth a wife, findeth a good thing.

As I stated earlier, please don't go 'awe' looking for him. Listen! This thought just came to mind. If you make up your mind to stay celibate (No Sex Before Marriage, for those of you who didn't know), if you make up your mind to keep yourself out of bed with any man before marriage, I believe that your knight in shining armor or night on a white charger has just mounted himself on his horse and has just started riding your way. Now, I don't know how far he must come or when he will arrive, but just be ready when he comes 'awe' grinning and 'awe' giggling like a Chinese mule stealing Japanese rice. Keep in mind ladies, you must be in control of the initial approach because most men will not be, no matter how hard they try. Remember, you are the one most likely to be left with a baby and no man. Don't get carried away and drop your panties momentarily, only to watch him drop out of sight permanently. However, in many cases, they didn't drop out of sight permanently because of another dumb invitation.

He is supposed to be an idealized chivalrous man, who comes to the rescue of a woman in a difficult situation. Do what you're supposed to, and you will be his woman and not just another woman. After you are married, he can honestly say,

1. She's not just another woman.
2. She's giving me a new born birth.
3. I've found sweetness on this bitter earth.
4. She knows the things to say, to help me drive my troubles away.
5. When the words she says won't do, she'll try a little kiss or two.
6. And if her kisses fail to move me, she'll take a little time to soothe me.

7. She knows how to console me.

8. She knows how to control me.

9. She taught me the meaning of giving.

10. She brought me back from the dead to the living,

11. From a one room dirty shack, she even washed the clothes on my tired aching back.

12. She's got electrifying loving, as warm as mother's oven.

13. Don't know where she gets the power.

14. Her loving gets stronger by the hour.

All because you're not just another woman. Now, if you don't wait until you are married, then you'll be like any other woman. Yep, another statistic in his political cabinet, his musical lyrics of lust. Love means going on with the one you love physically, spiritually, emotionally, and mentally where you will go with no one else. There's no need to expiate past issues like people will expect of you, trying to make atonement for your pass. I've already strongly made reference to these splenetic, intractable, unbending, compromising villains. It is, by far the inner sadness that causes other people to downgrade your relationship, and they cannot do that without downgrading the characteristics, the loving congenital and affable attributes of your mate. I'm almost certain about life being far more beneficial to them if they were to be freed of their inner hurt and miserable despair.

You know, one of the better words that can be poured from the pits of the 1,000,000 words of the American language is, 'biased' which means: unfairly prejudice for or against someone or something. In this case, someone. It has been said in many times pass that all men are dogs. Well, 'twinkle-twinkle little star, let me tell you something that comet from afar.' Dogs need dogs to make puppies. I know that came as a shocker.

Did you know that men need women to make babies? Men are really supposed to be more in control than women. It is overly obvious that women are just as bad because of the many cases in which there are any number (from 1 to who knows how many) of children and not knowing the father.

If you know your father, what good is it if he isn't there. Now the Bible says in 1st Corinthians 7:1, that at the time Paul was teaching on sexual immorality, that it is good for a man not to touch a woman.

Being the Master of biology and all physiological view, God obviously knew what he was talking about. With the brain being not only in the head at the top of the body, but the head of the body, it is the biggest sex organ in the body, which is the mind. Anything physiological has to do with the body and its system, you might notice your physiological response to a scary movie; notice how the heart beats faster and your hands get sweaty. We know that this branch of biology deals with the functions and activities of living organisms and their parts, including all chemical

Affable: pleasantly easy to approach and to talk to; friendly; cordial; warmly polite

and physical processes. The reason for God saying what He said about 'touching' is because the brain controls the body's production of the feel-good hormone dopamine. The more you stimulate her mentally (especially by touch), the more dopamine her body produces. This is what makes a woman lower her guard, insecurities, and her uncertainties. She's ready to act abnormal now. The touch has been a little too much for her to fight back, for now she is at the point of no return and he has found the beginning.

Her sex drive has soared into the clouds. Hopefully, she won't be pregnant when she has mentally descended. Dopamine has been referred to as the cupcake addiction. The dopamine in the brain is the one chemical that always seem to stand out because dopamine is the molecule behind all of our most sinful behavior and secret cravings. Some say dopamine is love, adultery, motivation, and addiction. The reality is dopamine is the top motivator behind all of this, but dopamine is none of this, which makes you responsible for your actions. Keep your hormones in check. Remember that in school? Keep your hormones in check? It can prevent a lot of future misery, such as, hardworking women, with many children and no man who constantly tell the children how sorry and lazy the man is. Yeah, he was okay as long as the feelgood hormone dopamine was being released; because of its able function to send chemicals from neurons to neurons. My theory from what I have studied and concluded is that lesbians and homosexuals are really suffering from chemical and neurons malfunction, yet an intentional malfunction. Remember, you are in control when you want to be. Neurons functions the same as free radicals in your body, playing practically the same role, except the role of free radicals deals more with physical sickness, while dopamine and neurons deal more with mental behavior, but their functionality is the same. To the average doctor this information is no big deal, but to me, it was a mindboggling revelation.

Yes, dopamine is that neurotransmitter which helps control the brain's reward and pleasure centers. It helps to regulate movements and emotional responses and it enables us not only to see rewards, but to take action- to watch them. Last, but not least, dopamine deficiency results in Parkinson's disease.

Now, have we been enlightened on this subject? Did God know what He was talking about? Do we understand why God wants us to control ourselves? We must not get carried away with a little too much touch. Amen! Amen!

So, a lot of touching, especially sex before marriage, does not guarantee long lasting, formal pledge, and spiritual obligation until death do us part. Sex before marriage doesn't mean that you know a person the way you should know them. It has nothing to do with the guidance of the Holy Spirit, but everything to do with the evil spirit.

Now, some may say, "Well, I don't know about all of that." Well, I say you don't need to know, if you trust God. You don't need to know, but we do need to obey. I'm not looking for a quick Amen, that's if I get one at all. No, you don't know, and the good thing about it is, God didn't tell us that we had to know, just trust. Why are we so afraid to get married without having sex first? Do you know that the number one ingredient for the recipe of fear is the unknown? No matter how many other ingredients, it is the unknown that makes this dish of fear complete. Just remember, it is God's way of guaranteed success, if we just trust and obey Him by taking Him at his word. Amen!

The Bible says, "*For God did not give us the spirit of fear but of power, and of love, and of sound mind* (2 Timothy 1:7, KJV). Notice, it's the spirit of power and of love and of a sound mind; not of imagination, but sound mind.

Spirit of Imagination

I am reminded of another educational truth, and I mean true story when a woman invited another woman who was not her friend in bed with her man. Not her and her husband, but her man only. She did it by giving her the spirit of imagination.

The spirit of imagination just came as a free gift while the wife was telling some other woman how good her man was in bed. In less than 48 hours, one woman who was listening and her imagination quickly became a souped-up fantasy that resulted into reality. How could she be upset after taking her personal bedroom business in this sweet, loving, and peaceful Philadelphia bar? Many times, bars have been the comfort stop and the hangout for broken relationships. There are a lot more people in bars with broken relationships than there are people starting new relationships. The bars are no place for a new relationship because of so many 'one-night flings.'

Ignorance and stupidity today can generate a lot of tomorrow's aches and pains. Now you are living in the sorrow of your last relationship and total fear of the next. The thought of a new relationship for some people in relations to marriage, is absolutely terrible. Not horrible, but terrible because terror has a direct act on people; not just to frighten or intimidate, but also to harm. It generates a feeling, mood, or ambience in horror that you might get from a scary movie. That's why they are called horror movies. It plays only with the imagination to see how people will respond. Terror, my friend, is the highest level of fear and grief is the lowest level of sorrow. To grieve has resulted in many cases- suicide. I understand that any 'one thing' in particular does not affect everyone the same way and my heart goes out to those who wasn't able to overcome the sorrow of that magnitude, but some of the suicides for the particular reason of a broken relationship; for me, would have been more commonly referred to as 'Star-Spangled Joy.'

Hey, if you are with the wrong person, it won't be long before that relationship is a perfect mess. And it takes an imperfect person to make a perfect mess. That's right, because perfect people wouldn't qualify, simply because there aren't any. Sad to say, but suicide is nothing more than an act of pride. It says that you have a better solution than God has. Now the Bible states in Proverbs 29:23 that, "A man's pride should bring him low, but honor shall uphold the Humble in spirit. When you make decisions without consulting your spouse, it relieves you of the responsibility of agreement, or at least you hope so.

Decision-making is not yours to be carried out alone. You're in this battle together now. It can be vehemently rewarding if you choose to have it that way. Let me say one more thing about suicide and hopefully not damage your theological insight. There are some doctrine and ideologies that has been taught in times past, that everyone that commit suicide is automatically lost.

New Birth

The Bible says in 1 Peter 1:3-5, "Praise be the God and the Father of our Lord Jesus Christ. In His great mercy, He has given us new birth into living hope through the resurrection of Jesus Christ from the dead (4) and into and inheritance that can never perish, spoil, or fade. This inheritance is kept in heaven for you, (5) who through faith are shielded by God; power until the coming of the salvation that is ready to be revealed in the last time.

Ephesian 1:13-14, "In whom you have also trusted, after that you heard the word of truth, the gospel of your salvation, in whom also after that ye believed, ye were sealed with that Holy Spirit of promise (13). Which is the earnest of our inheritance until the redemption of the purchase possession, unto the praise of His glory."

So, the Holy Spirit in us, is God's seal of promise and inheritance. That means the teaching of suicide means all souls are lost is the most doltish and vacuous teaching ever witnessed, or heard of. If there is a breakup between your spouse or your mate, try not to let it take you to that level of depression. Many of these academic, bookish, pedagogic, intellectual, heavyweights can be mighty convincing, if you are not careful; that is with information in general.

On Sunday, May 1, Betty and I were under attack, one week before Mother's Day. One of Betty's friend was told by Betty that we were getting married, but we weren't together at the time (not in each other's present). She claimed to be Betty's friend. She knew my ex, but only knew my name and maybe a little about me, but not enough to approach me as foolishly as she did. It was a vehemently oppositional approach, as if I was supposed to answer her. She deliberately and despitefully (not knowing how to act) questioned what she already knew and I knew she wasn't ignorant to the fact. Now, I had no choice but to ask, "Do you know what ex-wife means? Are you that naïve?" Are you that mentally artless?

Artless: without effort or pretentiousness, natural and simple.

It was obvious that she wasn't visually impaired. I couldn't have used a better word. This detainment, unsolicited, unsought, unrequested display of Christian ignorance came on such a childish level that a two-year-old would have seen right through those forty-two (42) years of unprogressive primitive Baptist living.

Obviously, no teaching, asking me something like, "Where is your ex-wife?" She asked right in front of my fiancé. If I thought you really wanted to know, then I would tell you, but because of your unconnected peevish spirits; I do not wish to discuss her whereabouts or her well-being. Just by looking at her, I saw much, much more to be concerned about, and I mean concerning herself.

Well, I guess you are reminded of my earlier statement about my zero tolerance for the splenetically despiteful. If we are to be concerned with the relationships of all relationships, which is

God our Father, our Lord and Savior Jesus Christ, and being led by the Holy Spirit to adhere to and operate in concert with His Concepts. I really, really believe that we will find our Christian lives far more rewarding which will generate much more lovable living. Amen! Amen!

Remember, a true relationship with Jesus Christ means not having to spend a miserable, agonizing, and excruciating eternity in the congregation of the unsaved dead.